For the Gemini Trust, Daughters of Charity
and Action For Development

E is for Ethiopia copyright © Frances Lincoln Limited 2010
Text copyright © Ashenafi Gudeta 2010
Photographs copyright © Ashenafi Gudeta, Betelhem Abate, Atakiti Mulu and Dama Boru 2010
Published in association with The Catholic Fund for Overseas Development

CAFOD
just one world

The Publishers wish to acknowledge Ifeoma Onyefulu as the originator
of the series of which this book forms a part.
Ifeoma Onyefulu is the author and photographer of *A is for Africa*.

Translations by Sara Ibrahim

First published in Great Britain and the USA in 2010 by
Frances Lincoln Children's Books, 4 Torriano Mews,
Torriano Avenue, London NW5 2RZ
www.franceslincoln.com

British Library Cataloguing in Publication Data
available on request

ISBN: 978-1-84507-825-6

Set in Vega Antikva

Printed in Dongguan, Guangdong, China by Toppan Leefung in February 2010

1 3 5 7 9 8 6 4 2

E is for ETHIOPIA

Ashenafi Gudeta ▾ Betelhem Abate
Atakiti Mulu ▾ Dama Boru

F
FRANCES LINCOLN
CHILDREN'S BOOKS

Author's note

My country is one of the oldest civilizations in the world. It lies in East Africa, set in a landscape of mountains and rivers, and the Blue Nile rises in Lake Tana. Our wildlife includes giraffes, lions, elephants, zebras, crocodiles, hyenas and all kinds of beautiful birds.

Ethiopia is rich in history. It has an important place in both the Christian and Muslim religions, with all kinds of colourful festivals. Thousands of people visit our ancient churches and mosques each year.

Ethiopian people follow many different traditions, make music in a variety of ways and speak several different languages. We love to dance, sing and have fun, especially on public holidays! Our food is spicy and delicious. The coffee bean originated here, and we hold a special coffee ceremony in which the aroma of roasted coffee, the incense we burn, and the pleasure of meeting each other all make for a unique experience. Ethiopians are a good-hearted people, and I feel blessed to be a part of this land.

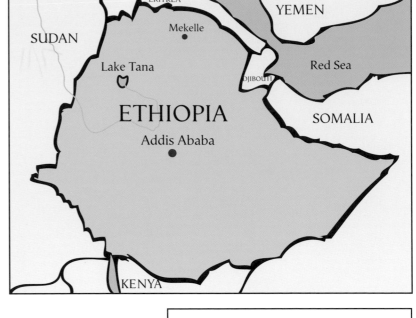

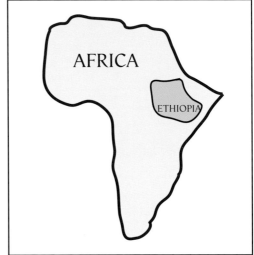

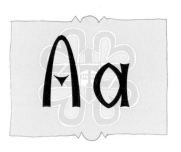

is for Aheya – a donkey. We use donkeys to carry goods between our homes, our farms and the market. You see them everywhere, even on the streets of our capital city, Addis Ababa, loaded down with wood, grain and water.

 is for Basket, used for storing grain and clothes, for sieving flour and for serving food. Women and girls weave them from the long, flexible grasses which grow in the fields and decorate them. When they're on sale in the market, they make a colourful sight.

is for Coffee. Ethiopia is the birthplace of coffee and it is our biggest export. To make this wonderful drink, we roast coffee beans in a pan and pound them to a powder. Then we add boiling water to the powder in a pot and let it stand for a while before pouring out the coffee. This is when we relax and exchange ideas!

is for Dancing. Ethiopian people like to express their strength and bravery through dance. Each part of the country has its own special dance, but the most popular one is the Eskesta or Shoulder Dance.

is for Ethiopia, a mountainous land in east Africa. It is thought to be the cradle of humankind, with an ancient civilisation and a history dating back 3,000 years. The 85 million people living here speak many different languages, and Amharic is our national language. Over half of us are Christians, and there are many Muslims as well as other traditional religions.

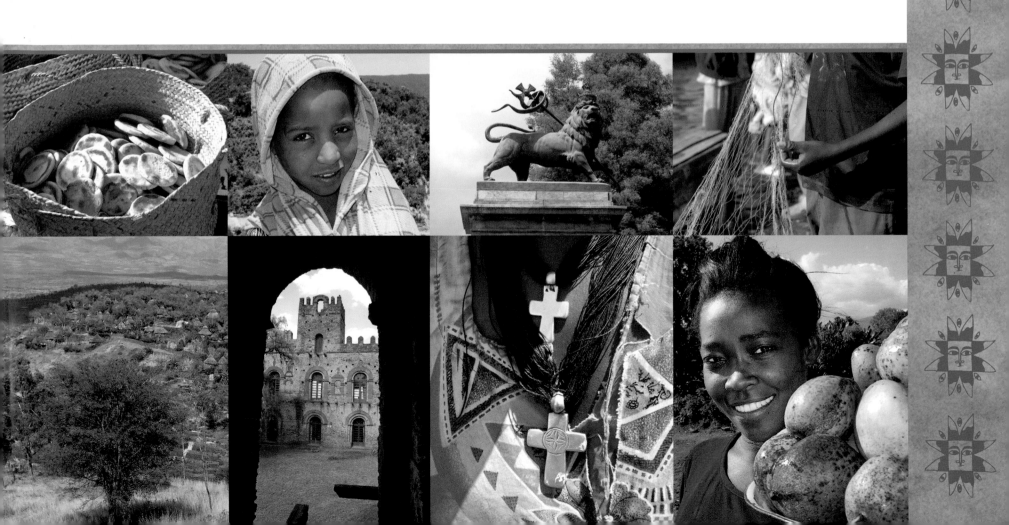

is for Injera – a round, flat bread we love to eat,
made from grain and baked using a special clay oven.
Just baked, it has a sour taste, but dipped in sauce
it is delicious! Injera is full of iron and keeps us healthy.

Jj

is for Jelebia, a long Arab robe worn by Muslim men and boys. Jelebia are worn on Muslim holy days and on Fridays, when Muslims make their way to the mosque for prayers.

is for Kitfo, a tasty, minced-meat dish that we eat with injera or *kotcho* (a kind of banana-root bread). We eat the spicy, oily meat raw or cooked, especially during Meskale, the Orthodox Christian holiday when we light bonfires to celebrate the finding of the True Cross on which Jesus Christ died.

is for Listro – a shoe-shine boy. Many young boys start their working lives in the shoe-shine business and work hard throughout the summer holidays. Some listros work full-time and do not go to school. You will often see them in the streets with their wooden box of polish, shoe-brush and polishing cloth.

is for Merkato, an Italian word meaning "market". Merkato is our commercial centre in the heart of Addis Ababa, the biggest marketplace in Africa. Everything is sold here: fresh vegetables, grain and groceries, livestock, traditional and modern clothes, handicrafts – you name it, you find it here!

N is for Net, used for catching fish in our lakes. You can often see fishermen by the waterside making their big, square nets, using *katcha* (sisal) or plastic rope.

is for Old. Fasilides' Castle, in the city of Gondar, dates back to the 17th century. Founded by the great Emperor Fasilides, Gondar was once our capital city, famous for its painting, poetry, music and religious study. It has many visitors.

P p is for Priest – an important person for Orthodox Christians. Priests preach the words of the Bible and lead prayers, as well as looking after our churches. Each priest wears a long robe and white turban, and carries a wooden or silver cross.

Q q

is for Quoda – a wooden jar used by the Borana people in the south to store milk. It is decorated with leather. Borana people eat a lot of butter and milk, and are well known throughout Ethiopia for the animals they breed.

is for Running. Ethiopia is home to many famous long-distance runners such as Haile Gebrselassie, Abebe Bekila, Deratu Tulu, Mesert Defar and Kenenesa Bekele. Each year Ethiopia hosts the Great Ethiopian Run, in which people of all ages and nationalities take part.

is for Shuruba – the traditional art of hair-braiding. Two past Ethiopian rulers, Emperors Tewodros and Yohannes, were famous for their braids. Many women and girls have their hair specially done for high days and holidays.

is for Tana, the largest lake in our country. Fed by three rivers, the lake is the source of the Blue Nile river and its great waters flow into the spectacular Tis Abbai Falls and power a hydro-power station. Lake Tana is dotted with small islands, some with ancient churches and monasteries.

is for Uniform. Students and schoolchildren have to wear a uniform to school, and you will see many different styles throughout the country. Some uniforms are blue, while others are red, green or black.

is for Veil. Muslim women wear veils to cover their hair and face. Some women are veiled in black from head to toe, while others wear lighter veils in grey and brown. In the streets of Addis Ababa, only very religious women wear veils.

is for Weha – water. We drink
it, wash and swim in it, and
use it to grow food and cook
our meals. In the countryside,
where supplies of drinking
water are hard to find, some
people dig a well in the ground
like this one, and collect water
in buckets, while others share
a communal tap and queue
to fill their water containers.

is for Xmas, which we celebrate on January 7. This is when men and boys play a traditional game called Genna – a bit like hockey. An Ethiopian legend tells how the shepherds looking after their flocks played Genna to celebrate the birth of Jesus.

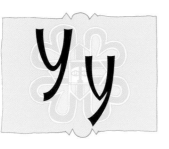

Y is for Youth. In the countryside, young people work in the fields or stay at home farming and herding animals. In the city, most youngsters go to school and have spare time in the evenings to dance, play football or watch American movies!

Z is for Zenbil, a shopping bag which women everywhere carry to market. It is woven from palm leaves to make it strong, then decorated with dyed palm leaves. Nowadays zenbil are often woven from plastic and they look lovely and bright.